NINJA REALMS OF POWER

SPIRITUAL ROOTS
AND TRADITIONS
OF THE SHADOW WARRIOR

STEPHEN K. HAYES

CONTEMPORARY
BOOKS, INC.
CHICAGO ▪ NEW YORK

Photos of meditation sequence and
Ninpo Taijutsu by Gregory Manchess.

CONTENTS

This book is lovingly dedicated to
Marissa Christine
who entered this world as I began the completion
of this volume
and a new phase of my own personal growth,
and who will always have
a place in my arms,
no matter which realms she is destined to explore.

INTRODUCTION

This volume is a look at the spiritual roots that were but a part of the complex cultural and historical phenomena that intertwined to produce the art of the ninja shadow warriors over a thousand years ago in Japan. During my years of apprenticeship in Chiba Prefecture, Noda City, under ninjutsu grandmaster Masaaki Hatsumi, I became fascinated with the spiritual systems that are generally accepted to be part of the foundation of the personal survival system known as *ninjutsu*. Some of these more influential spiritual traditions are described in this volume for the benefit of those who desire more depth in their exploration of the art of ninjutsu, the cultural history of Japan, or the universal role of individual spiritual experience in any society.

It should be mentioned, however, that the training and disciplines described here in the sections on *sennin* Taoist mountain immortals, *mikkyo* esoteric Buddhism, and *shugendo* mountain power cultivation are not the only roots of ninjutsu. This volume is not in any way meant to imply that these systems in their pure and complete forms are to be considered as ninjutsu training itself, or that they are required to be studied as part of ninjutsu training. This volume is intended to describe some of my own explorations into the spiritual roots of the warrior tradition, because I myself felt compelled to make these explorations. Anyone else wishing to study the art of ninjutsu, as taught in Masaaki Hatsumi's Bujinkan dojo, will have to draw his own conclusions as to whether he wishes to go on to

ix

a study of these spiritual disciplines in their freestanding forms.

As is the warrior tradition of Japan, the spiritual tradition of the Rising Sun nation is steeped in centuries of fascinating lore and outstanding personalities. It would please me to know that perhaps through this volume Western world readers might gain a more thorough understanding of ninjutsu's significance as a unique product of ancient Japan's rich culture.

1 QUEST OF THE WARRIOR
THE ELEVATION OF THE SPIRIT

Over the past few decades, the word *warrior* has increasingly played a part in Western world culture. The word itself can have many definitions, depending on an individual's political, economic, and religious frame of reference. On one extreme, a warrior is seen in the limited scope of the Western definition as a fighting man or, literally, as one who wages war. On the other end, a warrior is defined in the broader Eastern sense as one who engages the world, or one who willingly seeks out the challenges of living, as opposed to remaining in the sanctity of the family home.

Proponents of the Western definition can cite the extreme cultural mood swing that has taken us from the naive and charming idealism of the 1960s to the gritty and alarming demands of just two decades later. The age of group action to clean up "the rest of the world" rather than our own backyard has given way to a perhaps harder-edged reliance on personal responsibility and accountability for the quality of life as we experience it as individuals. The newer credo states that if we all clean up our own backyards together, the rest of the world will be in great shape as a direct result.

As the world's conventional power relationships and legal values have begun to crumble at the edges, individual citizens can find themselves caught in a bind emotionally and financially. We are alarmed to find that the original pioneer spirit of the North American continent has slowly and surreptitiously given way to the comfort of letting others in our corporation, union, church, political party, and special interest group do the thinking and planning for us. We are then devastated when caught unawares by a factory layoff from a position we had assumed was secure for life, a political scandal in which respected government figures are exposed as criminals, or a television exposé that shows the political and commercial aggression of several popular religious figures posing as ministers of spiritual salvation. Small bands of hysterical murderers blithely terrorize the citizens of the free world without any fear of retribution in return. Western juries regularly hand down severe financial punishments to their peers in the community for going "too far" in the defense of their homes, property, and loved ones while under violent attack from criminals who willingly chose to inflict harm and disruption on the lives of their victims.

It is small wonder that the lure of the warrior has returned at least in movies if not in actual lives. The frustrated, confused, and beleaguered citizen can turn to the warrior for vicarious satisfaction. Rambo-like heroes, with ludicrous loads of firepower slung across their massive naked backs, single-handedly defeating evil legions, regularly play counterpoint to films of trickster heroes (à la Indiana Jones) who single-handedly foil sinister plots to dominate the world. Even more emotionally appealing is the fact that it is often "the Establishment," or some manifestation of a heartless corporate conspiracy, against which the lone hero must contend for his life. Is it any wonder, then, that the ninja mountain rebel of Japan, with his reputation as an unstoppable fighter and a power-wielding sorcerer, has come to be considered the ultimate lone warrior of film and fiction?

From the opposite end, the word *warrior* has also gained a new, nonviolent respectability. Meditation classes, sales and management workshops, wilderness survival seminars, personal encounter sessions, Native American retreats, and even diet counseling therapies have been including the concept of warriorship in their packages. This less-than-warfare definition is not at all a deviation from the original meaning, as developed by the ancient spiritual disciplines of the Himalayan region. In this tradition, there were said to be two ways to seek enlightenment; these were known by the Sanskrit terms for *warrior* and *householder*.

The warrior-aspirant left the comforts of his home and went out to seek enlightenment by trial. By immersing himself in the world and facing all confrontations, the spiritual warrior conquered his fears and learned of ultimate truth through his successful accomplishments.

The householder aspirant, on the other hand, withdrew from the complexity and excitement of the world to search for enlightenment from within. By cutting off all that could distract him, the spiritual householder gained the insights of ultimate truth by cutting through the illusion of worldly dictates and demands.

Somewhere between the one-man armies' rampages and the abstractions

Warrior training that does not acknowledge the grander significance and symbolism of the struggle to overcome personal limitations that block the path to enlightened consciousness is not true warrior training.

in the businessman's edition of the *Book of Five Rings* lies the experience of warriorship to which I was apprenticed over half a lifetime ago. In the tradition of the ninja phantom warriors, the disciple must be willing to approach warriorship from both extremes at the same time. From this viewpoint, then, warrior training that does not include facing actual danger is not true warrior training at all, but merely a desire to play at being bold. By the same viewpoint, warrior training that does not acknowledge the grander significance and symbolism of the struggle to overcome personal limitations that block the path to enlightened consciousness is not true warrior training either, but merely mechanical experiences in how to further wound the world that we all must share.

To honestly go beyond the use of the word *warrior* as a label for one's pet pastime, the individual must bridge the span between extremes. The true warrior must prove himself in physical confrontations and must understand that his fighting techniques are merely vehicles for gaining a higher level of mental and physical power. It is more common, and easier, for most to dwell in one extreme than to command the entire spectrum.

Much has been written concerning the physical training methods of the various Oriental combat arts. This, of course, is right and natural, for physical training is a necessary first step on the journey of warriorship. Ultimately, however, there is a "spiritual" side to the warrior arts as well. This is the realm about which very little has been written.

The term *spiritual*, unfortunately, can be confusing to many in the Western world. As with so many other concepts that we import from the East, it is tempting to force the idea into our Western world view. If it is not physical, it must be beyond or outside or the opposite of physical, conventional logic wants to dictate to us. However, we can use the term *spiritual* to label those aspects of our physical world that defy our powers to describe them in a mechanical context. Ultimately, everything is physical (or mechanical), in the sense that everything that exists must have some foundation upon which its existence is based. Culturally, we tend to label "spiritual" those indefinable things around us that cause us extreme overwhelming awe or intense feelings of powerlessness and inferiority.

To deal with those haunting aspects of life that are impossible to understand or control through scientific and rational means, we humans have constructed our various religious systems, through which we work to come to some sort of peace with the unknowable. Therefore, when we hear the word *spiritual*, we most often think in terms of religion.

Unfortunately, religion often works to shrink and tame the very wild and mysterious forces that first drew our wonder. In the process of making the inexplicable safe for the masses, the possibilities for real illusion-piercing insight become reduced. One might say that they are only available to those who dare to ride the breaking crest of direct life-altering experience. The warrior learns of the spiritual realm by dwelling on the cutting edge of the sword, standing at the edge of the fire pit, venturing right up to the edge of starvation if necessary. Vibrant and intense living is the warrior's form of worship.

It is also curious that the spiritual traditions of both the Eastern and Western worlds seem somehow at odds with their stereotypes. The Western world, with its emphasis on materialism, rational logic, and scientific validation, is characterized by three primary religions that all rely on a doctrine of absolute faith in a cosmic diety; this system exists outside of the believer and is impossible to verify through empirical research. One can see that Judaism, Christianity, and Islam have a common base of total and unwavering faith in the invisible. The Eastern world, on the other hand, with its emphasis on the intertwinement of fact and feeling, is characterized by a doctrine of inner and outer consciousness. One can see in the teachings of Confucianism, Taoism, Buddhism, and Shintoism the necessity of understanding the role of the individual in the workings of the universe. The irony is that the rational and scientific West has developed the spiritual systems of faith, while the mystical and intuitive East has developed the spiritual systems of mental contemplation.

It is easy to quibble about which of the two approaches is "right" or "better." Such comparisons are, of course, pointless, since both stands merely reflect the deeply ingrained cultural patterning of Western and Eastern life. This patterning is so deeply rooted in the individual psyche that it is extremely rare for an individual to recognize it. The pattern dictates its own reality and rigidly negates the realities of the other patterns. The Christian sees the Taoist as a wayward heathen, while the Buddhist believes the Muslim irresponsibly avoids cultivating his own enlightenment.

The patterning, of course, can occasionally break down, causing an individual to immerse himself in the details and fashions of an opposing realm. Midwestern American youths suddenly adopt white turbans, exotic diets, and Himalayan names to replace what perhaps they think of as the

Ususama Myoo-oh, the symbolic patron spirit of the Henshoji Shugenja seekers of enlightenment in the wilderness.

mundaneness of their previous existence. Across the ocean, Japanese young people convert to Western religions, adopt Latin names, and let go of the traditions of their forefathers. This form of behavior is often more a manifestation of boredom or discontent than a true understanding of the spiritual depths of another culture.

Extremism in either form, whether blindness to other cultures' wisdom or blindness to our own culture's wisdom, is the effect of limited thinking. True power in life comes from exploring and accepting all realms in which we can cultivate something useful. The ability to transcend the limits of culture seems easier to come by now than it was in ages past. As a result of the revolutionary impact of modern communications media, people have more opportunity to see the grander picture of the world today. It is in this framework that we as warriors venture into the arena of life, willing to be affected and elevated by all we experience.

The warrior tradition embodied in the art of ninjutsu is a unique manifestation of the power of the spiritual quest when forced by military, political, and economic events to deal with worldly concerns. Ninjutsu was not at all developed as a martial art for the sake of martial arts; rather, it was forced into existence by the demands for survival faced by the mountain families dwelling on the edges of conventional feudal Japanese society. The art of the ninja was the product of a wide range of intellectual and experience sources. To truly understand it, one must thoroughly study a thousand years of Japanese political, cultural, and religious history. Like so many other things Japanese, the ninja's art is a blend of influences and a reflection of ever-changing needs.

From such Japanese spiritual traditions as *shugendo* seeking of power in the mountains, *mikkyo* secret doctrines from the far-off Himalayan kingdoms, *sennin* Taoist practices for the goal of immortality, Shinto animistic identification with the spirit inherent in the natural phenomena around us, and a host of other Japanese folk belief systems came the body of knowledge eventually known as ninjutsu, the art of accomplishment through invisible action. When the military dictatorships of the twelfth through seventeenth centuries moved their samurai troops against the resistance of the mountain dwellers southeast of Kyoto, they were met with a system of survival tactics unlike that of any other enemy. Based on an intimate knowledge of the forces of nature and of the nature of humankind,

In this stereotypical caricature of the historical ninja, the mystical warrior carries the scroll of his ancestors' wisdom, symbolic of the spiritual transmission of the knowledge that has kept his family alive for generations.

The warrior learns of the spiritual realm by dwelling on the cutting edge of the sword, standing at the edge of the fire pit, venturing right up to the edge of starvation if necessary. Vibrant and intense living is the warrior's form of worship.

En no Gyoja, legendary seventh-century founder of the Shugendo practice of subjecting oneself to harsh rigors on sacred mountains as a way of attaining the very power of the mountains themselves.

The Japanese written characters for *bu gei sha*, or warrior, combines the kanji letters for "martial," "art," and "person."

The kabuki actor Danjuro, dressed for his famous role as Benkei the monk, the powerful yamabushi guardian of the ill-fated Minamoto no Yoshitsune.

The author trains in Japan with his mentor, Dr. Masaaki Hatsumi, thirty-fourth grandmaster of the Togakure ninja ryu.

The wrathful Fudo Myoo-oh, often depicted as the patron overseer of the warriors of ancient Japan.

*When the military dictatorships moved their samurai
troups against the resistance of the mountain dwellers
southeast of Kyoto, they were met with a system of
survival tactics unlike that of any other enemy. Based
on an intimate knowledge of the forces of nature and of
the nature of humankind, the subtle combat skills of the*
shinobi *warriors were refined while the enemy remained
baffled for centuries.*

the subtle combat skills of the *shinobi* warriors were refined while the enemy remained baffled for centuries.

In the world of the shinobi spiritual warrior, the realm of the spirit provides for tangible physical results, just as the physical world is the stage for developing the power of the spirit. The two realms are not opposites; they are two distinct views of the identical process. Ninjutsu, born of these two parallel worlds, draws its strength from both ends of the spectrum.

Unfortunately, no discussion of the spiritual realm would be complete without at least a mention of the so-called dark side of spiritual power. Indeed, the original ninja families of Japan were often described by the fearful as practitioners of magic and sorcery. Such accusations, of course, sprang from ignorance and superstition as well as the accusers' arrogant belief in their own superiority. Just as fears of sorcery and witchcraft once spurred on countless officially sanctioned murders in the Western Hemisphere, the original ninja of feudal Japan were persecuted and referred to as "less than human" by those who feared and resented them.

Since the ancient ninja families had everything to lose and little to rely on if forced into conventional battle, it must be admitted that many of the phantom warriors used their enemies' fears against them. If fear in the enemy's heart would assist the ninja families in protecting their villages, then fear was a weapon used right along with the sword. If the sight of a black-clad phantom reciting a foreign sutra, with his hands knotted in bizarre patterns, gave the conventional enemy some misgiving, then of course the ninja would rely on the very power to frighten that the enemy had handed over to him.

Ultimately, of course, there is no such thing as a "dark side" of power. The only thing dark is the choice to apply power for purposes that would further splinter the potential for oneness in the universe. That which works to promote separateness as opposed to connectedness in the spiritual as well

In the Japanese Shinto tradition, the dynamic spirit of nature is seen as a manifestation of the divine. Here, a weathered miniature shrine sits atop a rock of special spiritual significance.

as physical realms is what the Buddhists call *mara* and the Christians call *evil*. Beyond the twisting of power into a tool for inappropriate personal promotion at the expense of the grander universe around us, however, the higher truth is the fact that universal laws are universal; that is, all natural laws operate because they exist and all laws of nature operate equally efficiently for all agents of nature. The only difference between one who knows and one who fears, therefore, is a lack of knowledge and experience on the part of the fearful. Ironically, even this rudimentary knowledge is included in that wisdom that cannot be known by the morally timid, and therefore, is impossible for the willfully fearful to accept.

Despite the phenomenal advances of science and thought in the five hundred years since the ninja were most savagely persecuted, these same irrational fears still surface far too often. Just as in ages past, modern religious fundamentalists still cling to their own narrow definitions of what is "right" for us and "wrong" for others. More often than not, the label of "wrong" is applied to anything having to do with the implementation of personal power and responsibility in life, or the enjoyment of the natural pleasures provided to us.

Unfortunately, as in ages long behind us, those who would explore the total power that lies within themselves have to face the displeasure of those who have been trained to suppress personal power. That resistance too is part of the spiritual warrior's battle. Indeed, it could be argued that after all the fighting and struggling and clashing is behind us, the slimy yellow-eyed dragon of ignorance will be looked back upon as the most insidious and threatening of all the foes we faced.

2 SENNIN
STRADDLING THE
TWO AS ONE

The Tibetan monk who had escorted the Dalai Lama to Japan sat cross-legged before the small crowd of which I had managed to be a part. The man had been an abbot of a temple monastery when the Communist Chinese invaded his homeland, and decimated his country's culture, twenty years previously. Following his lecture on the power of the spirit to overcome the negative tendencies of the personality, the lama asked through his interpreter if there were any questions that he could answer for us.

I asked the holy man his opinion on whether enlightened consciousness could be created through the deliberate avoidance of any potential conflict or confrontation. The seeker is approaching enlightenment, the lama had explained, when he can see through the illusion of negative or splintering emotions such as jealousy, anger, greed, hatred, and fear. What if, I asked, I leave behind all persons and things that could cause grief in my life? Perhaps I could go off to live on a mountain somewhere. In my seclusion, there would be no enemies to make me feel threatened. Living alone, or surrounded only by a small group with whom I shared acceptance and love, I could be spared the experience of jealousy, anger, hatred, and the like. Would that, however, be the true budding of enlightened consciousness, or merely the hopeful illusion of spiritual unity?

The Tibetan holy man cocked his head to the side and smiled broadly. Through his interpreter he commented that mine was a difficult but important question. The Japanese monks in attendance silently waited for the Tibetan's answer.

Such an approach to enlightenment was a good way to begin, he stated. Divorcing oneself from those elements that would distract one from the purity of consciousness that he sought was a fine first step. In Tibet, as in China and Japan, the practice of extended retreat from the world was a common practice for religious aspirants.

The former abbot leaned forward as though to speak in confidence. Through his translator, he whispered his warning: "Be careful with such training. The power of intention, guided by the altered perception that sees no obstruction, can create its own realities," which seem to transcend the dictates of conventional natural laws. Such insights can become intoxicating and addictive. "This is fine," he said, "so long as the seeker remains on his secluded mountain, ensconced in his carefully constructed realm." Should he ever attempt to reenter the world of everyday reality, however, he would find himself stripped of the powers he had come to be convinced were his eternally. Unless the returning seeker were extremely cautious, such a shock could have literally fatal results.

Stemming no doubt from the tales of Chinese mountain hermits who lived to cultivate supernatural powers and discover the keys to immortality, Japan's *sennin*, or "mountain recluse," lore has been a part of Japanese culture for over a thousand years. In the fantasy accounts of the tradition, the sennin Taoist immortals were said to dwell in the clouds, possess the powers to control the laws of nature, summon incredible animal allies, predict the future, and even heal diseased mortals. Perhaps more historically accurate are accounts that the sennin hermits dwelt in remote, cloud-ringed peaks and engaged in a form of Taoist meditation and yogic practice that lead them to extremely refined and heightened sensitivities.

The sennin renounced the everyday world of tension, strife, and conflict for a tranquil life of simplicity, quietude, and the harmonies of nature. This characterized the beginning stages of his quest for the power to transcend the confining limits of time and space. Based on timeless *omyodo* yin and yang polarities, mountain mysticism, arts of divination, shamanism, and folk witchcraft, the sennin hermit's regimen for the cultivation of immortality covered all aspects of daily living. Unencumbered by the demands of conventional working life, the lone sennin was free to pursue the refined disciplines that would bring him to an intimate knowledge of the workings of natural law.

Since much of the sennin's wisdom came to him through direct experience as opposed to theoretical study, dogmatic intellectualization was rejected in favor of direct, subjective perception. Choosing the richness of personal subjectivity as opposed to the seeming dryness of universal objectivity, the sennin often dealt with reality through the means of spiritual

Text continues on page 22.

A Taoist Sennin Breathing Exercise

The purpose of this exercise is to become more aware of the subtle energies that are carried in and radiate out from the spinal column. At the very core of the human body, the spine is the central axis from which all energy channeling direction must flow.

Pick a pleasant and undisturbed setting in natural surroundings. Sit in a slightly downhill direction if possible. This will make it easier for your hips to form a relaxed base for a naturally erect spine. Fold your legs in front of you, bringing the sole of your left foot to rest against the inside of your right

thigh and pulling your right leg in toward the shin of your left leg. Take in a deep and slow breath, totally filling your lungs and extending your spine upward. Enjoy the feeling. You may want to lower your chin slightly in order to straighten out the vertebrae of your neck.

Choosing the richness of personal subjectivity as opposed to the seeming dryness of universal objectivity, the sennin often dealt with reality through the means of spiritual symbolism. Impressions were couched in the guise of the familiar, and personal power often took the form of separate agencies from nature.

Lower your fists to the ground beside your seat and push downward to straighten your arms. Feel your arms lift your body upward until your torso is hanging from your uplifted shoulders. Maintaining the lift, concentrate on feeling your vertebrae separate, lifting skyward and sinking earthward at the same moment. Imagine what it would feel like to actually grow several inches in height just by letting go of the tension that contracts the muscles of your spine. Drop your seat onto the ground gently and repeat the exercise for a total of three repetitions.

Rest the palms of your hands on your hips in a light gripping hold. Starting from a centered position with an erect spine, lean out to your right side, feeling the leaning motion snake itself up your spine in a wavelike ripple. As your torso naturally returns to the central balance position, allow yourself to lean out toward your left side with the same snaking ripple of motion up your spine. Again return to the central position and repeat the exercise for a total of three repetitions.

Place your hands palms down on your thighs, just above your knees. Starting from a centered position with spine erect, lean forward from the center of your torso as though someone had grabbed you by the solar plexus and pulled you forward. As with the previous exercise, you should feel the motion ripple upward from the ground to the base of your skull. As your torso naturally returns to the central balance position, allow yourself to lean backward from the center of your torso as though someone had pushed you backward with pressure against the front of your solar plexus. Use the same ripple effect as you go backward and return to the central balance position. Repeat the exercise for a total of three repetitions.

Suspend your arms in the air at your sides and rotate your torso gently to the right. When your body has gone as far as it can go without straining, lower your right palm to the ground behind you and press the back of your left wrist against your right knee to provide just a little more twist to your spine.

Return to the central balance position slowly and reach around with a twisting motion to your left side. Use your hands as before to increase the twisting action before returning to the central position. Repeat the exercise for a total of three repetitions.

Now that you have "awakened" your spine and physically reminded yourself that what we call the backbone is actually constructed of many individual bones, hold your torso in a naturally erect posture and shut your eyes. Breathe deeply and slowly, allowing your stomach to expand and contract naturally as your lungs fill and empty. As you breathe in, be aware of the positive vitalizing force of the air that expands your lungs. Imagine that you can actually consciously experience the infusion of oxygen into your bloodstream. As you breathe out, be aware of letting go of the negative exhaust elements that would work to limit you if you retained them.

Imagine that you are drawing some of the stabilizing force of the earth's electromagnetic energy upward into your torso. Like the mercury that rises in a thermometer degree by degree, the energy in your spine rises and expands out a few inches at a time. With each breath out, imagine that you can feel the earth's stabilizing and invigorating energy rise another inch up the center of your spine. With each breath in, imagine that you can feel this force expand and radiate out. Continue this exercise in visualizing and feeling for the energy as it slowly moves all the way up your spine to the base of your skull. Hold the full feeling of energy as long as you can, then rise quickly and go about your daily chores.

Text continues from page 16.

symbolism. Impressions were couched in the guise of the familiar, and personal power often took the form of separate agencies from nature. This shamanistic influence is seen in the ancient legends and artwork about the sennin. Special and unusual abilities were often attributed to fantastic animal allies or spirit guides that aided the sennin. Famous sennin characters were often identified more by their spirit allies than by their own personalities. Gama Sennin is known for his alliance with a large, three-legged white toad. The toad is no ordinary amphibian, but the personification of the very life breath that is shared by all creatures. Tekkai Sennin is often portrayed in the act of blowing or whistling his spirit out of his body, his gourd flask of magic potions at his side. Kinko Sennin is portrayed as traveling on the back of a magical flying carp, and often is depicted as a beautiful courtesan riding on the back of a carp while studying a *maki-mono* scroll of personally transmitted wisdom. Chokaro Sennin's constant companion is a white mule that can carry him thousands of mile in a day. According to legends, the mule was kept in the form of a folded paper scroll when not required for travel, and brought to life with a sprinkling of water

To go with the Tao, or follow the path or way, was the key to advancement. "What is is," they would state, and to attempt anything in conflict with that ultimate reality was misspent energy already doomed to result in frustration and failure.

whenever the antigovernment-recluse Chokaro required his services.

Of key importance was the focus on physically and spiritually transcending the limits of the corporeal body. The Taoist *dokyo* practice combined various disciplines of physical conditioning and meditation. Practices involving yogic sciences, breathing exercises, dietary considerations, and sexual energies concentrated on the refinement and transformation of the body. Complementary practices involving meditation, visualization, projection of consciousness, and extrasensory experience concentrated on the development of the spiritual factor. When blended, the two extreme manifestations of the human life force, the earthlike body and the heavenlike spirit, were reflected in each other as shown in the symbolic *in* and *yo* (*yin* and *yang* in the Chinese language) that make up the Taoist *taikyoku* graphic swirl of counterbalancing dark and light polarities.

This interactive harmony of body and spirit is the sennin's living reflection of the constant balancing relationship between the fundamental extremes of the universe, or the concepts of maleness and femaleness on the vast cosmic scale. The Judeo-Christian tradition speaks of the symbolism of heaven and earth, the Japanese esoteric Buddhist tradition speaks of the *kongokai* diamond thunderbolt spiritual realm and the *taizokai* matrix womb material realm, and the Western scientific field of electromagnetics uses the concept of negative and positive to describe what are in effect the same values. The female *in* is reflected in the negative (−), dark, heavy, earthy, wet, finite, contracting, and lunar. The male *yo* is in turn reflected in the positive (+), bright, light, heavenly, dry, infinite, expanding, and solar.

In the teachings of the sennin's dokyo, it is explained that prior to the beginning of all that is, there existed only the vast potential of all that could or would be. Often referred to as the void in the metaphysical systems of the Orient, this potential existed as a single thought or germinating cause. Over three thousand years ago, the inhabitants of rural mountainous China conceived of this void as the *Tao*, or "way." This Tao could be translated as "what is," or that which is the ground of actuality. According to the beliefs of the Japanese sennin and their Chinese Taoist forerunners, to fight

Text continues on page 26.

The Japanese written character for *sen* (left), of *sennin*, is made up of the two lesser characters for "human" and "mountain," giving the combination character the meaning of "hermit" or "religious recluse." The *nin* (right) of *sennin* is translated as "person."

The Taoist taikyoku graphic symbol. The swirling polarities are not so much the opposites of each other as reflections of each other. *In* becomes *yo* which again becomes *in*, all as a consequence of the observer's changing perspectives.

The Japanese written character for *in* (left) originally was a reference to the cooler side of the mountain that received no direct sunlight. *Yo* (right) was a reference to the side that was in a position to receive direct sunlight and was thereby warmer. The two written characters later adopted the larger significance of the general polarities that are commonly thought of as opposites.

艶中八仙
琴高

丁子屋内
雛鶴
つゝの

歌麿筆

The Taoist immortal Kinko, in the form of
an elegant courtesan riding a magical carp.

The Taoist immortal Tekkai Sennin blowing out his spirit guide.

Text continues from page 23.

the Tao, or to struggle against what was meant to be, was the height of folly. To go with the Tao, or follow the path or way, was the key to advancement. "What is *is*," they would state, and to attempt anything in conflict with that ultimate reality was misspent energy already doomed to result in frustration and failure.

The word *void* is actually a bit misleading to Westerners, for whom it may have connotations of *containing nothing* or, even more confusing, *ineffective or useless*, as in a voided contract. Perhaps it is clearer to use the English word *devoid*, in the sense of the ultimate potential being devoid of any specific manifestation, shape, or meaning. Since there is no manifestation of what is to be at that point, there is only the potential of what is to be.

From this initial stage of total inclusivity, or *taikyoku*, emerged the existence of the fundamental polarities. The Taoist sage Lao Tsu writes of the oneness of the Tao becoming the duality of the yin and yang (in and yo in the Japanese language). The written characters originally used to convey the yin and yang concepts were the Chinese characters used to refer to the dark, cold, and wet side of a mountain peak as opposed to the bright, warm, and dry side of the same peak. Thus, the polarities themselves are nothing concrete and separate, but are merely different perspectives of the same mountain peak. In their symbolic roles as representations of the general polarities, the yin and yang of the Taoist metaphysics likewise reflect polarities in perspective rather than polarities in opposition.

The sennin works physically and mentally at consciously experiencing the bridging of the gap between the in and yo elements around and inside of him. By coming to understand the symbolism of external realities, he thereby brings himself ever closer to bridging that gap between body and mind, intellect and feeling, and the physical limits of the spirit as opposed to the spiritual limits of the body. He learns to transcend the illusion of the "ten thousand things" (the infinite things in the universe as distinct and unrelated to each other) and gain the grander vision of the universe as a single unified process as opposed to an overwhelming collection of seemingly conflicting and unrelated parts. No longer overwhelmed, the sennin then becomes the immortal, free to play with the natural laws that only work to confound the conventional thinker. After attaining the vision of all-as-one, the sennin is then free to see from the vision of all, feel from the touch of all, and move with the power of all.

3 MIKKYO
BINDING THE
THREE AS ONE

It was evening and the summer sky had long been dark by the time Koyu Tanaka and I reached the entry of the temple run by the priest we had driven over eight hours to visit. Here in my friend's boyhood home on the shores of the Sea of Japan, in this small village in Yamagata, I would meet the man who had first introduced my friend to the essence of *Mikkyo*, or the "secret knowledge" of the Himalayan teachings as they had been cultivated in Japan for over a millenium.

From the mystical teachings of Mikkyo came the ninja's insight into the workings of the universal scheme, and from the application of this understanding came the ninja's personal power. The compendium of teachings known as Mikkyo has its roots in the esoteric tantric lore of India, the southern stretches of the Himalaya Mountains, and, to a lesser degree, China. In the early part of the ninth century, Japan was introduced to these concepts through such monks as Saicho and Kukai, who traveled to China to study the Indian works as taught by sages there. Mikkyo teachings of power and magic also arrived with the wandering Chinese monks, shamans, and hermit priests who fled their native land at the collapse of the Tang Dynasty.

During my years of training in the dojo of my warrior arts teachers, I had been introduced to certain concepts of physicalizing the intentions of the

The Mikkyo temples of Mount Koya, sacred
site of Kobo Daishi's mountain monastery.

The monk Kukai, posthumously known as
Kobo Daishi, who introduced ninth-century
Japan to Mikkyo teachings through his
Shingon, or "True Word" or "Mantra,"
tradition.

spirit. The ninja's *kuji goshin ho*, or "nine-syllable protection method," had
been derived from the original *zomitsu* nonreligious Mikkyo that had
filtered into Japan from China over thirteen hundred years ago. Through
this practice, the spiritual warrior worked to unify the sometimes quarrel-
some elements of body, intellect, and will. I had always heard references to
the religious Mikkyo, and although it was not required for our training in
the ninjutsu school, I was curious to explore the roots of what we did
practice.

The monk Saicho, posthumously known as
Dengyo Daishi, the older contemporary of
Kukai, was responsible for the transmission
of the Mikkyo esoteric doctrines through his
Tendai tradition.

The priest's home was built right onto the side of the temple and extended into a small garden of gnarled trees and rambling azalea bushes. Through the blackness of the night, I could see a dim light from behind a rice-paper *shoji* screen in the side wall of the priest's living quarters. The softly lighted panel had an indescribably warm feeling to it. I was experiencing a feeling that could best be called nostalgia, although indeed I had never visited that place before.

The wood-and-glass latticework door rattled sideways on its rusty tracks,

The man who feels himself the weaker of two contenders is the one who will let go of all considerations for others and adopt the extreme of savagery as his only defense. Tools of power provide means. It is up to the bearer to provide the perspective to use them wisely.

squealing out a greeting to the interior of the house. As was the Japanese custom, I first opened the door and stepped into the entryway of the house before I called for the attention of the householder. I reflected with wry amusement on how an American homeowner might react if he found a visitor wandering through the front of his house and calling out his name.

The little priest greeted us in the main room of the dwelling. With much joyous bowing and animated conversation, the holy man and my friend Tanaka-san renewed their boyhood comradeship. I was introduced to the priest and was warmly welcomed. I could tell that the man's face was a permanently happy one, and I was surprised to be greeted by this cheerful person, who reminded me more of a tavern keeper than a teacher of closely guarded, esoteric Buddhist ritual.

My friend Tanaka-san had been given the name Koyu during a retreat ceremony in a *Shingon* Mikkyo temple years before I had met him. He gave up his original name for this new one as a symbol of his commitment to seeking the truths of a higher realm of reality in everyday life. He had shared with me what he could from his own studies. When my questions had gone beyond his own experience, he had agreed to return to this village with me, where I might learn more of the "secret doctrine."

Over small, steaming cups of pale green Japanese tea, the three of us examined five swords from the priest's private collection. The gracefully curving blades glowed in the golden overhead lighting. In as polite language as I could find, I mentioned that I found it somewhat contradictory by Western standards to find this priest with a collection of tools crafted for the purpose of taking lives.

Patiently, the Mikkyo priest pointed out that the blade was forged for the purpose of protecting the sanctity of life. The cutting edge afforded the bearer that reserve of confidence and power that permitted gentle and courteous behavior. The man who feels himself the weaker of two contenders is the one who will let go of all considerations for others and adopt the extreme of savagery as his only defense. Tools of power provide means. It is up to the bearer to provide the perspective to use them wisely.

The kongokai mandala, symbolic of the pure
spiritual truth of the ultimate actuality of the
universe.

Such was the power of the Mikkyo secret doctrines, the pleasant priest
went on to point out. I was surprised, to say the least, by the abruptness of
his comparison. I nodded my head silently when he asked me in a quiet
voice whether I would like to see his temple sanctuary.

In stocking feet, the three of us moved single file along a narrow
passageway that snaked its way over a darkened garden at the rear of the
house. Wordlessly we moved along the smooth wooden planks and
eventually entered the smoky, cavernous room that housed the priest's
treasure.

Before me in the dim light reclined a huge wooden Buddha, on his side

The taizokai mandala, symbolic of the
personal material experience of the reality of
the universe.

with his legs extended a full twelve feet beyond his hips. Parts of the statue's textured surface had been rubbed to a glossy slickness in testimony to the legions of faithful who had entered this sanctuary over the centuries. Beyond the gently smiling wooden face I could see a second Buddha figure, this one seated with legs folded and framed by golden leaves hanging from the ceiling, which was invisible in the blackness overhead.

I was awed by the massive reclining statue, if not for the religious significance, then at least for the monumental craft that created it. The priest playfully patted one of the statue's toes and commented that he did that for good luck. Not one to turn down any opportunity for increasing my fortunes, I too patted the toe on my way around the statue, which I now realized was stretched between two huge paintings.

*Through each thought, word, and deed, the seeker of enlightenment further imitated the chosen **Buddha***, *or "awakened one," until the imitation eventually transformed itself into the actual state of enlightenment.*

I moved closer to one of the paintings. Yards wide and towering above me, it carried the faces and stylized bodies of hundreds of little characters that seemed to radiate out from a central figure. I turned around and looked across the room at the other *mandala.* Its collection of figures seemed to follow a progression of nine squares laid out end to end and side to side.

The priest explained that the mandala paintings provide two distinct views of the makeup of the universe. Each represents one of the polarities of the universal process, the material and the spiritual, and are contrasted to help the seeker understand *why* and *how* the universe operates the way it does. In actuality, both mandala designs reflect the same thing, only from the two distinct perspectives. Of course there is only one universe, in the sense that the universe is the total collection of all that is. It is only our limited human perspectives that create the two radically differing concepts of physical and spiritual. In a like manner, we can only see either the inside of the temple or the outside at any given moment. Though the views are radically different, there is indeed only one temple.

The taizokai mandala represents the "matrix realm," *matrix* here meaning "womb," or that within which something originates and takes form. This stylized work of art represents how a human sees his universe as though he were the only center. All perception and realization radiates from the me-as-center, and all-around-me takes its place within the universe.

The kongokai mandala represents the diamondlike hard, cold reality of the ultimate form of the universe, in which we as individuals each play our small role. All individual perceptions aside, there is the ultimate scheme of totality that flows on timelessly, blending all actions, thought forms, and essences to produce what we might call cosmic history.

In more mundane language, the kongokai diamond realm could be seen as the vast stretch of eternity in which we experience the years of our own lifetimes, and the taizokai matrix realm could be seen as the fraction of the instant in time that we refer to as the current moment. Each perspective reflects the other, for, indeed, life as we experience it is a series of ever-unfolding current moments.

I moved between the two mandala to peer at the weathered and time-aged black-and-gold countenance of the image that faced into the sanctu-

Kannon, the personification of the forces of compassion, merciful taking-all-into-the-one, and protective nurturing in the universe. Present in all aspects of the universe, Kannon is formless and appears in various male and female guises. Technically, Kannon is a *bosatsu*, or *bodhisattva*, a potential Buddha that has temporarily forsaken the opportunity to dwell in permanent enlightenment in order to aid others in their search.

The Sanskrit mantra for the taizokai Dainichi personification. Adding to the depth of the symbolism, the mantric power phrases can be employed in the written form as well as the spoken form. Even in Japan, the original Indian Gupta script is still used.

ary. From its lofty position against the wall farthest from the entry doors, the statue commanded a view over the heads of all who entered here. The little priest commented that the statue was of Kannon, referred to in the Western interpretation as the goddess of universal mercy.

I learned that words like *god* or *goddess* were difficult to deal with in this priest's frame of reference. Strictly speaking, Kannon is not a goddess in the sense of being a power outside the human realm to whom supplicants pray and bid out of need. Kannon is rather to be seen as a particular emanation of or given quality of the universal process.

Certainly, the priest acknowledged, there were those less-sophisticated persons who derived comfort from addressing Kannon as a living spiritual protector. Talk of universal schemes and such was of little significance to some of the local people who regularly visited the temple.

Ultimately, Kannon is the personification of that aspect of the universe that could be described as nurturing and sheltering, providing a pulling-together of hearts and encouraging the benevolent qualities of all that exists. Kannon is that quality that looks out across eternity through tear-filled eyes of compassion to see the endless suffering of humankind. By futile clinging

The *chiken-in*, or "wisdom fist mudra," of Dainichi Nyorai. With this example of ketsu-in hand posturings, the practitioner assumes the mudra of all-encompassing universal enlightenment in order to attain sight in distant places and other times, thereby gaining freedom from the limits of time and space.

to ignorance in the form of the will to eradicate one another, ever more straying from the possibility of realizing the oneness that is the grander truth of the universal process, humankind further increases the burden of that essence that is referred to as Kannon.

The priest told me that he did not necessarily pray to the statue, as I had mistakenly thought, but rather, he studied the statue in a meditative nonverbal way. The statue was to be seen as a three-dimensional symbol of the dawning of universal compassion in the heart of the beholder. One not so much petitioned the force of Kannon as strived to actually embody it.

This total merging with a given force is the essence of the secret doctrines, I was told. One lived daily with the task of identifying with the chosen image in all levels of awareness. One spoke like an enlightened aspect of the universe, one held one's body and moved like an enlightened aspect of the universe, and one filled one's mind with the vision of an enlightened aspect of the universe. Through each thought, word, and deed, the seeker of enlightenment further imitated the chosen *Buddha*, or "awakened one," until the imitation eventually transformed itself into the actual state of enlightenment.

The practice of merging through imitation on all levels of awareness is referred to as *sanmitsu*, or "three secrets" or the "triple secret." In the ancient Himalayan tradition, the three-level transformation procedure involves the highly symbolic use of gestures, spoken words or sounds, and detailed mental images. Through the use of *mudra* (*in* or *ketsu-in* in the Japanese language) finger-entwining, which sometimes can involve total body posturing as well, the practitioner works at creating the physical symbol of that which he or she seeks to become. Through the use of *mantra* (*jumon* in the Japanese language) power words or sounds, the practitioner

Ancient graves at the site of Kobo Daishi's Shingon sect headquarters on Mount Koya, in the wilderness of Wakayama Prefecture.

Koyasan mountain's *Oku no In*, the final resting place of ninth-century scholar Kobo Daishi, the founder of Shingon-shu esoteric Mikkyo. Not actually described as a grave, the Oku no In is said to house the transcendent Kukai still in meditation, awaiting the coming of Miroku, the Awakened One of the future.

Naritasan Temple shrines to Fudo Myoo-oh, showing Fudo's huge sword on the left of the staircase.

works at calling the name of or speaking the identifying phrase of that which he or she seeks to become. Through the use of yogic *mandala* (*mandara* in the Japanese language) explicitly detailed mental images, the practitioner works at seeing a symbolic sequence of events-to-be that will take him toward experiencing that which he or she seeks to become.

In the Mikkyo of the Buddhist world, the practitioner selects or is given a personification of one particular Buddha, or "force with the power to awaken," which he or she works to identify with intimately. By physically imitating the given Buddha through a symbolic mudra, speaking like the given Buddha through a symbolic mantra, and willfully conjuring up the image of the given Buddha through symbolic mental visions, the seeker works at making his or her experience of the given Buddha a reality. The ultimate goal is to move, speak, and perceive like the chosen Buddha to the point at which one actually embodies the force of that Buddha.

In the secular world as well, the Mikkyo sanmitsu process is equally as valid for creating new realities and attaining desired results. In the worldly realm of the warrior, the pure spiritualism of the given Buddha image is replaced with the slightly less noble image of any desired outcome. The warrior then completes the three-fold process of the sanmitsu realization. He or she engages in action that will cause the goal to be realized, speaks in a manner that ensures the goal being realized, and visualizes himself or herself in the situation of having the goal realized. It is then merely a matter of having physical reality catch up with what is determined to be.

The aspirant who wishes to become an accomplished warrior must engage all three points of the sanmitsu triangular base. He must physically surround himself with role models who are superior to him in warrior accompishment, thereby physically spurring him on through effective and well-directed training activities. *This is the body of the goal.*

Mentally and intellectually he must train himself to use the thought processes and speaking style of the accomplished warrior, even if only in imitation at the beginning. *This is the speech of the goal.*

Finally, he must thoroughly believe in the inevitability of himself as the accomplished warrior. In his mind, in his heart, at the very core of his soul, he must feel that this is indisputable. This intention must be so strong that it actually changes the aspirant's perceptions of physical reality. *This is the thought of the goal.*

With such powerful tools granted to virtually everyone, the compelling universal question becomes not so much *how* do we accomplish our dreams, but rather *why* do so very few of us go on to create resplendent living temples out of ourselves?

4 SHUGENDO
BINDING THE
FOUR ELEMENTS AS ONE

The hot summer wind at our backs, Rumiko and I worked our way up the steep slopes of Omine Mountain. The sun beat down on us mercilessly as we climbed toward the flattened clearing that sat at the foot of the stone stairs leading up to the Hinshoji temple. Miles of wooded terrain surrounded us, and far beneath the tumbling peaks stretched acres of flooded rice fields in the rural region northeast of the city of Kumamoto.

We had traveled from our home in Rumiko's family compound along the shores of the Ariake Sea to be a part of the day's fire ceremony. The ceremony would take place at the remote Hinshoji sacred grounds and would mark the opening of the region's shugendo mountain training season. Arriving early in order to converse with the shugenja who would be conducting the ceremonies, we were greeted with quiet bows from the white-kimonoed attendants who were scurrying about to prepare for the open-air fire ritual.

As was the custom for such rituals, we received several split cedar sticks imprinted with the Sanskrit character for *vahm*, the so-called seed sound necessary for invoking the protective aspects of the shugenja's patron overseer, Fudo Myoo-oh. One of the flat nine-inch sticks was to ensure family prosperity, one was to cover peace and harmony in life, one was directed toward safe travel. Noticing Rumiko's maternity smock, a smiling monk handed my wife another piece of wood—for the safe delivery of our second daughter, which she carried inside her, he informed us cheerfully. We painted our names on the sticks and handed them back to the shrine attendant.

Inside the Henshoji structure, we faced a wall of Fudo Myoo-oh statues and figurines, placed there by well-wishers and seekers of enlightenment. Often they stopped here before departing into the wooded wilderness to search for keys to the ultimate universal understanding. The Fudo figures all clutched small upraised swords in their right hands and held coiled ropes in their left. The fierce little faces with intense eyes and jutting teeth all seemed to be staring down at us. Not at all meant to be a god, the Fudo Myoo-oh character is regarded more as an imaginary saint that provides an example for our subsconscious minds to emulate. Not to be worshipped, but to be imitated, the resolute Fudo represents those aspects of the universe

It was reasoned that the earth-grounded human being could take on the heaven-charged aspects of superior energy through extended contact with that energy. Those original seekers who wandered the peaks thought to house the divine Mikumari no Kami were said to take on the very power of the mountains themselves.

that encourage and enforce the proper progress of fate, the unhindered and meant-to-be scheme of totality. In the little figures with their halos of flame we see the potential for all human beings to center their resolutions on personal growth in harmony with the inevitable.

A tall tower of hardwood logs began to take shape in the open courtyard below. Within hours, that tower would be ablaze, eventually producing the searing coals that would constitute the test of faith for the stony-faced shugenja monks. In imitation of the resolute and unmovable Fudo Myoo-oh, they were to tread barefoot across the embers. Young practitioners dressed in the traditional pale yellow costumes of the *yamabushi*, "mountain seekers of power," were weaving pine boughs into the log structure. An older assistant wearing an orange version of the billowing pantaloon *hakama* skirt tied at the ankles worked beside them. With his animated conversation and happily boisterous spirit, this older assistant played an interesting counterpoint to the serious and deliberate younger men.

The practice of shugendo shamanistic power cultivation is as old as the recorded history of Japan itself. Said to have been created by the legendary En no Gyoja, also referred to as En no Otsune, in the early seventh century, the practice is a blend of oral teachings, visualized emulations of symbolic power figures, physical tests of courage and conviction, and experiential work toward the gradual accumulation of mountainlike personal power.

It is believed that the roots of the shugendo tradition lie in the ancient belief that the mountains were the dwelling place of Mikumari no Kami, the spiritual protector of agriculture. Certain mountain stretches were thought to harbor powerful forces in their surrounding atmospheres, as was often evidenced by the unusually high amount of lightning in those regions. Persons wishing to elevate their own "charge" moved through those regions, where they could come into contact with the supernatural energy levels.

Electrical charges work to balance themselves out. Weaker stores are made stronger through contact with stronger sources. Therefore, it was reasoned that the earth-grounded human being could take on the heaven-

The Japanese characters for *shugendo* (at left) are made up of three symbols that combine to read "the way to enlightenment by means of the cultivation of mastery." The wrathful Fudo Myoo-oh (above), symbol of the resoluteness with which the universe plays out its grand and unwavering scheme.

charged aspects of superior energy through extended contact with that energy. Those original seekers who wandered the peaks thought to house the divine Mikumari no Kami were said to take on the very power of the mountains themselves. From this ancient practice, it can be seen how the reverence for Mikumari no Kami and the ancestral spirits developed into the *Shinto*, "Divine way," system, and how the reverence for the individuals who traversed Mikumari no Kami's dwelling place developed into the *shugendo*, "enlightenment through accomplishment," system.

Since there are no written creeds or doctrines in shugendo, it is difficult to ascertain its exact origins or theoretical slants. It is thought that the original roots are a blend of related spiritual practices, including *zudagyo* Buddhist teachings, *dokyo* and *omyodo* Taoist philosophies, the *zomitsu* nonreligious forerunner of Mikkyo doctrine, Shinto, *jukkyo* Confucian teachings, and a wide assortment of Japanese folk beliefs. Later, the practice of shugendo did adopt some aspects of other formalized religions, including some of the written tracts of Tendai Honkakuron, Sanno Ichijitsu Shinto, and Ryobu Shinto. The practice always has been an experiential development process, however, through which individuals work to tame

Shugenja and yamabushi were regularly used to gather intelligence, carry messages, deliver payments, and assist in negotiations made difficult by great distances that sometimes spanned enemy territories. Shugenja priests and shamans were sought out as well for their abilities to provide power incantations and blessings over fortress sites, military equipment, and weapons.

forces of nature in order to gain mastery over them. The principles are taught through immersion in the experience.

Rumiko inquired of one attendant as to whom we might question for more detailed information on the practice of shugendo. The monk explained in a friendly fashion that we were fortunate that day, for we would have the opportunity to learn of the shugen practice from the Daiajari himself. The *Daiajari*, or "great adept," was considered to be a living treasure among those who sought enlightenment through the yamabushi experience. Well over eighty years old, the Daiajari would be the senior-ranking participant in the day's ceremonies. He had come at the invitation of the local Kancho, head of the Kumamoto area Omine Mountain *dojo* training area. The man with whom we spoke pointed toward the group preparing the fire tower, and my wife and I turned to look.

There before us was the same group of young and middle-aged shugenja supervising the construction of the bonfire base. Their older assistant still scurried here and there, tucking in pine boughs and arranging ropes. I turned back to the monk and back to the group once again. Incredulous, I realized that the older "assistant" in the orange leggings and the white undershirt was the only one old enough to fit the Daiajari's description. I had expected the revered "great adept" to be seated in aloof contemplation somewhere, preparing for the moment at which he would emerge to begin the proceedings. I had not expected that this "living treasure" would be the one laughing and scampering and throwing himself at the bulk of the hard labor just minutes before the ceremony was to begin.

The Daiajari interrupted his work to welcome us with a beaming smile. Surprised to be so suddenly confronted with the ultimate authority on the practice I had for many years sought to explore, I groped to put my questions into words. The little man continued to smile pleasantly and gaze at me as though he had all the time in the world.

The true seat of shugendo practice was located on the Omine Mountain

The procession of yamabushi wilderness
power seekers ascends the hill to the
courtyard of the Henshoji temple.

The Daiajari and his young attendant
prepare for the ceremony.

Traditional conch shell trumpets sound a
wailing salute to announce the beginning of
the *goma* fire ritual.

The *Kancho*, or "training hall chief," reads
aloud a proclamation of his disciples'
intentions.

The practitioners of shugendo regularly subject themselves to the rigors of walking across fire, plunging through freezing waterfalls, and dangling upside down from ropes that hang over the sides of mountain cliffs.

that lay south of Nara on Honshu, Japan's main island. From the man's explanation, I had to assume that the Omine Mountain on which we stood outside of Kumamoto was a namesake for the central Omine that I had visited the month before. What little doctrine that existed in shugendo had described the central Omine peak as the point from which the yamabushi-aspirant would venture into the symbolic realms of the taizokai and kongokai. The taizokai "womb of the material realm" was said to be the Kumano region of the mountain. The kongokai "diamond of the greater

Before the staircase leading up to the Henshoji structure itself, the log and bough tower is ignited.

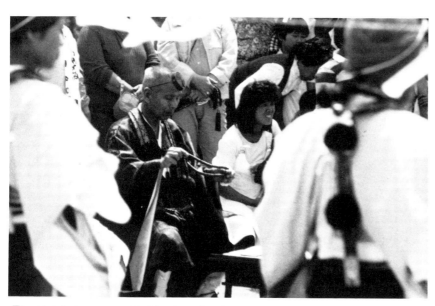

The Daiajari prepares his blessings for the
cedar *kogi* sticks that will carry the wishes
of the participants into the flames.

spiritual realm" was said to be the Yoshino region of Omine Mountain.
Since the mountain itself was to be considered a living mandala, all trees,
rocks, and living beings that inhabited the peak were considered to be forms
of divinity in their own right. The shugenja, or yamabushi, as they are also
known, used experiences in both realms to search for spiritual allies in
nature and, eventually, total enlightenment itself.

The powerful individuals who practiced shugendo had a major influence
on the arts of war as well as the shape of the island nation's religions.
During the feudal ages of Japan, the yamabushi had played key roles in the
military victories of such periods as Genpei, Nanbokucho, and Sengoku.
Shugenja and yamabushi were regularly used to gather intelligence, carry
messages, deliver payments, and assist in negotiations made difficult by
great distances that sometimes spanned enemy territories. Groups of
yamabushi from Yoshino, Kongo Katsuragi, Kumano, Hakuzan, Haguro,
and Hikuzan were often relied on for their intimate knowledge of mountain
trails and footpaths. The special political and military relationship between
certain shugenja groups and the ninja families of the Iga, Koga, and Negoro
traditions is also a documented part of Japanese history. Shugenja priests
and shamans were sought out as well for their abilities to provide power
incantations and blessings over fortress sites, military equipment, and
weapons.

In a graveled parking area below the elevated Hinshoji courtyard, the
procession of dignitaries had assembled and begun their slow climb up the

Smoke and flames leap skyward on a windy day.

From behind a veil of smoke, the Daiajari
tosses the sticks into the intense heat.

roadway leading to the ceremonial log tower. The long column of shugenja snaked its way upward, the aged Daiajari shielded by a huge red paper umbrella in the middle of the procession. His thin white undershirt had been covered with a brilliant orange silk kimono jacket that matched his leggings.

The entourage approached the courtyard and one of the shugenja used a *sanko* thunderbolt-handled sword to chop through a rice straw rope that cordoned off the ceremonial confines. The group entered the open sanctuary and formed a ring around the green tower as the supreme Daiajari and the hosting Kancho took their places on low benches facing the broad staircase that lead to the temple above.

The Kancho read the initiatory invocation from a scroll while the crowd prepared for the beginning of the fire ordeal. Conch shell trumpets sounded and ceremonial arrows were fired into the air. Symbolic combat with long-handled axes was carried out. Gifts as tokens of gratitude and hope were presented. As the box of signed cedar sticks was carried to the Daiajari, the signal was given to torch the log tower.

With a booming rush of heat, the bonfire ignited into a ball of orange-and-white flame. Quietly, intently, as though the billowing inferno before him were just an illusion, the Daiajari concentrated on putting his spiritual seal on each of the sticks that had been presented to him.

The charred logs soon began to collapse against each other, forming a pile of flaming rubble. The Daiajari began tossing the signed sticks into the heat of the center. Occasionally a glowing log would tumble from the pile

Shugenja in attendance push the glowing logs into the center of the fire.

to roll toward the ring of observers. The Kancho would casually walk over to the flaming plank, pick it up in his bare hands, and toss it back onto the pile. When the bulk of the lumber had been reduced to glowing coals, crews with poles emerged to crush and distribute the burning remains into a flat surface for the yamabushi to walk across.

The cheerful Daiajari rose and addressed the crowd. He spoke of how the majority of people fear, and therefore battle against, the very forces of nature of which they are a part. The shugenja overcome their fear by facing nature and working with it, thereby rendering the powers of nature into their tools. Symbolically, the threats of fire, water, and mountain are subdued through dangerous but confidence-inspiring rituals, freeing the seeker from the limits of fear. The practitioners of shugendo regularly subject themselves to the rigors of walking across fire, plunging through freezing waterfalls, and dangling upside down from ropes that hang over the sides of mountain cliffs. With no fears to unduly rob him of positive energy, the Daiajari put forth, the human is then free to move through life with a smile on his face and peace in his heart.

The Kancho's hands form a ketsu-in configuration in support of, and in coordination with, his visualized intention and mantra (words of power).

The tower of flaming logs is reduced to
intense red-and-white coals as the
participants prepare for their walk.

The Daiajari is the first to cross the glowing embers.

Quickly, before reason could prevail, I found myself pulling off my shoes and socks and scurrying to the end of the line.

The author crosses the flame bed as the
shugenja chant encouragement.

After completing a brief ritual in which the glowing embers were faced, the spry little man leaped onto the coals and actually stamped his way across the fire pit. Heat waves shimmered and danced around him as he charged in determined fashion across what must have been a searing expanse. In morbid fascination, I watched his feet for signs of injury.

The smiling Daiajari was then followed across the coals by the Kancho of the Henshoji temple and then the senior-most of the Shugenja in attendance. Some stamped their way across as had the Daiajari. Others flew quickly with barely settling feet.

As the determined monks made their way across the remains of the bonfire, the beaming great adept turned to where Rumiko and I crouched watching the spectacle. "Anyone else care to try?" he taunted with a happy grin and gleaming eyes.

Quickly, before reason could prevail, I found myself pulling off my shoes and socks and scurrying to the end of the line. My mind reeled in hesitancy as I considered what I was about to do. What if I had been too bold, responding foolishly to what had not been a real invitation but merely a pleasant jest? What if the others knew some inside information, some trick to prevent the burning of flesh on searing coals? What if their feet had been treated with some sort of chemical preparation? Perhaps there had even been some sort of hypnosis going on to protect them.

Time was running out. I stood at the edge of the pit, my bare feet shuffling along the sun-baked dirt. Forward was the only option open to me. I had been trained as a warrior of the body and spirit. I had faced other kinds of challenges, several that were far more dangerous than this. I took a breath and brought my palms together. I entwined my fingers into the *dokko-in* hand configuration of the *kuji no ho* spiritual protection system handed down by the ninja tradition. With conch-shell trumpets blaring, spiritual battle flags flapping in the hot wind, the Daiajari smiling and nodding in encouragement, I steeled my will and charged into the heat. Feet moving resolutely through the coals, wind moving effortlessly in and out of my lungs, my eyes on Rumiko waving at the end of the fire pit, I kept going. Emboldened by a new sense of power, I was thrilled by the experience. I began to grin and stamp just like the Daiajari.

I knew there was one less demon to get in my way from that day forward.

The Japanese written characters for *Bujin*, the "divine warrior," the symbol selected by grandmaster Masaaki Hatsumi for the name of his training hall.

The author with his ninjutsu teacher Masaaki Hatsumi.

5 NINPO TAIJUTSU
THE MEANS OF THE ENLIGHTENED COMBATANT

Koichi Oguri and I walked the snow-dusted streets of sleeping Noda City. For years he had been traveling all the way from Tochigi Prefecture twice a week just to train for a few hours in the dojo of Dr. Masaaki Hatsumi. After the evening's training, he would walk the deserted streets to the town's all-night movie theater and buy a ticket. Oguri-san would then spend the rest of the night dozing and watching the films until the first train left for his home the next morning.

I would ride the last bus of the night across the Edo River and through the countryside of Saitama Prefecture to my little house in Koshigaya City. The training hall that Koichi Oguri and I had chosen to attend was hardly convenient. But then convenience was low on our list of priorities. We were both pleased simply to have been accepted as students there. In the mid-1970s, the home of Masaaki Hatsumi was the only place on earth where one could find training in the little-known art of Japan's ninja.

Oguri-san and I talked of the art we shared. The man was many years my senior in the training hall, but this particular training hall was not run according to the strict formalities of a normal dojo. The uncharacteristically informal tone of Dr. Hatsumi's *Bujinkan*, "Divine Warrior," dojo worked to create friendships among the students, regardless of their respective ranks or years in training.

"Hatsumi sensei does not seem to use the concept of *genin*, *chunin*, and *jonin* ranks in the practice of ninjutsu anymore, does he?" I asked.

Once again, I was amazed to learn of the depth of the tradition to which I had apprenticed myself. There was always so much more than met the eye.

Historically, when the ninja families of feudal Japan were at the height of their power, inclusion in the ninjutsu tradition was determined solely by birth. The underground nature of the organizations prevented their true natures from being revealed to outsiders, and left only the offspring of the ninja themselves to inherit the family profession.

According to historical accounts, at the head of each family tradition or clan was a *jonin*, "high man," director or commander-in-chief. It was the jonin's responsibility to determine the alliances and strategies that would best serve his family's needs. In many cases during the most turbulent years of feudal Japanese history, the true identity of the jonin was concealed from the ordinary agents and operatives for security reasons. This precaution guarded against the possibility of government informers slipping into the organization and learning too much. It also permitted the jonin to observe the intricate inner workings of the clan without having to weigh concerns for personal safety.

Effortless natural motion that allows the attacker to make mistakes is the key to understanding the grandmaster's ninpo taijutsu. In this example, the author's kick is deflected by the grandmaster's leg.

Directly beneath the jonin family head was a group of *chunin*, "middlemen." Taking their orders directly from the jonin, these trusted field commanders were responsible for interpreting and implementing the family head's plans and strategies. The chunin knew how to get things done, and they were familiar with the individual strengths of the agents and field people on whom they could rely to get the job done. Taking the role of insulating go-between, the chunin also served to ensure the anonymity of the jonin, thereby reducing the threat of double cross or dangerous breaches in family security.

The *genin*, "low men," were the base of the hierarchy, doing what was necessary to protect the family. Possessing a wide range of combat and intelligence gathering skills, the genin agents were the ones who actually got the work done. Trained in survival skills from birth, the genin inherited a legacy of total service to their family's cause and to the welfare of their community as a whole.

Koichi Oguri shook his head in a way that indicated that the question was a difficult one. "Hatsumi sensei is really training us all to be jonin," he replied.

"Jonin? We are all expected to head up our own group of followers someday?" I was surprised at the man's answer.

"That's not the kind of definition I was referring to. Sensei is of the highest caliber of practitioner; therefore, he can only teach us from his elevated viewpoint. That is what jonin really means, in the esoteric sense."

I had previously learned that, contrary to my prior beliefs, the ancient ninja had rarely ever advanced in status. The son of a genin agent would naturally learn from his father the skills of the genin agent, and would in turn pass them on to his son if their family's survival depended on it. The chunin and jonin families operated in a similar manner. It was no different then from life today where individuals seem to be born into the level of society at which they will remain for life. Assembly line workers rarely ascend to corporate management positions, and those few persons who eventually assume the chairmanships of the major international corporations have usually been groomed for them from early life.

Oguri-san seemed to be stretching the concept even further. I asked what he meant by the "esoteric" or hidden sense of the definition.

"Technique and motivation can have a level of quality as well as the person who is involved in the art. The level of one's ninjutsu can be low, middle, or high in quality. That is what we mean when we refer to Hatsumi sensei's training us all as jonin."

Once again, I was amazed to learn of the depth of the tradition to which I had apprenticed myself. There was always so much more than met the eye.

As there were three levels of service in the ninja families of old, there were as well three levels of how the public understood the art of ninjutsu

Elimination of Superfluous Movements

Direct and unaffected motion as a means of handling dangerous situations is the key to effective self-protection. Therefore, the challenge to the spiritual warrior is learning to let go of unneeded actions that require too much energy. Like the sculptor who seeks to liberate the angel in the rock by removing just enough stone, or the *haiku* poet who seeks to summon a feeling through the careful pruning of unnecessary wordage, the combatant cultivates the power of simplification in movement. Letting go of unnecessary motions and actions, as opposed to struggling to memorize and hold onto complex strings of set techniques, is the approach to be taken.

In this scenario, the author defends against a straight punch to the face by allowing the aggressor's punch to fly on unhindered, right past the target. By subtly leaning out and forward, the defender adjusts his body angle so that the attacker thinks that the target is still there and does not stop or redirect his now-useless strike. As the attacker extends himself out into a vulnerable position, the defender straightens his arm and leans forward to allow the edge of his opened hand to slam into the neck of the advancing attacker. A step through while extending the arm into the attacker's neck snaps the attacker's head back and drives him backward. The beauty of this type of movement is that the defender can use precise timing instead of brute strength to defeat a determined attacker, since it is the attacker's momentum that really supplies the damaging power.

itself. The genin, or "lower ninjutsu," represents the misunderstanding of observers who chose to label these arts as treacherous, dark, and mercenary skills of sabotage and assassination. The chunin, or "middle ninjutsu," represents the impressions of observers who respected the ninja arts as comprehensive systems of personal combat and intelligence gathering. Above that, the jonin "higher ninjutsu" represents the realization that the art was a manifestation of a spiritual purity that permits harmony with natural laws and oneness with the universe.

In this example as well, the same philosophy of direct and unaffected motion can be seen in response to a slightly different attack. In this scenario, the author defends against a hooking punch to the face by allowing the aggressor's punch to fly on unhindered outside the target. By subtly leaning in and forward, the defender adjusts his body angle so that the attacker thinks that the target is still there and does not stop or redirect his now-useless strike. As the attacker extends himself out into a vulnerable position, the defender straightens his arm and leans forward to allow his own fist to slam into the face of the advancing attacker. A continuation of the leaning motion snaps the attacker's head back and drives him backward. As in the previous example, the beauty of this type of movement is that the defender can rely on precise timing and positioning instead of brute strength or raw speed to defeat a determined attacker, since it is the attacker's momentum that really powers the strike he encounters.

One's personal development in the ninja arts can also be considered on three value levels. If coming into harmony with the laws of nature is the ultimate goal of ninjutsu training, an ever-increasing ability to get things done with as little risk and effort as possible is the realization of that goal.

If a murderous conqueror were plotting to invade the ninja's community, the genin defender would rely on his incredible physical skills and honed senses to accomplish what others would feel to be impossible. The genin would attempt to gain access to the murderer and eliminate him before he could destroy the ninja's homeland.

In this third example, the author defends against an advancing rear hip throw by allowing the aggressor's tension and higher center of motion to create his own downfall. By subtly leaning out and forward, the defender adjusts his body angle so that the attacker's strength is redirected in such a way as to cause him to lose balance. As the attacker struggles to complete his throw, the defender simply alters the direction of his resistance and pulls the attacker backward with a forward rocking motion. The defender then crouches to follow the attacker to the ground, his open palm already in place for a crushing slam to the head. In grappling situations as well as striking, the defender can use the ease of precise timing and natural unstrained body motion to defeat a determined attacker, since it is the attacker's own momentum that really unbalances him.

In the same scenario, the chunin defender would call upon his superior intelligence and personal contacts to accomplish through others what must be done. The chunin would use his network of friends and associates to help him eliminate the enemy with as little personal risk as possible.

If the murderer should unknowingly plot against the jonin defender, there would be ultimately no need for any specific action on the ninja's part. The enemy would suddenly and coincidentally develop pneumonia and die before he even had a chance to mount an invasion.

In taijutsu unarmed combat, physical lessons to the student of jonin

Text continues on page 83.

Action as the Tool and Not the Goal Itself

Contrary to the apparent excitement involved in mastering the more acrobatic and athletic martial arts is the ninja's goal that "the less can overcome the more." Avoiding the more popular trends toward technical excellence and continuous physical conditioning, the ninja works to gain experience in defusing the danger rather than meeting it head on. Not one to engage in a slugging match for the mere sport of it, the ninja knows that to stay happy and healthy he must overcome his assailant in as direct a manner as possible.

The effectiveness and efficiency of the ninja's taijutsu approach, as opposed to that of the more traditional or popular martial methods, can be compared in this and the following examples of an identical attack. As the attacker lets loose with a straight jab to the face, the conventional fighter might be tempted to hold his ground and rely on the speed of his limbs to intercept the punch. This philosophy contradicts the principles of the ninja's taijutsu. Here, the defender ducks his head and shoulders to avoid the punch, causing him to exert himself just to return to a neutral ready-to-counter position. The defender next attempts a trapping movement, which is overthrown with a countertrap from the attacker. The attacker then exerts a twisting grab to pin the defender for the next round of attacks. Note that both attacker and defender stand in place, firing off countering salvos from stationary bodies that are also stationary targets. Note as well that there are just too many moves going on here for anyone to establish any real control over the outcome of the clash. In a game of skill like this, of course, the more skillful of the contenders will win. Therefore, as a game or sport, this sort of approach might be interesting or challenging, but as a system of defense against murderous attackers, it is extremely risky.

The goal is ever the attainment of true economy and naturalness in motion, and the ability to let go of inefficient methods.

The author demonstrates the natural total-body movement of the ninja's taijutsu method against an identical attack. As the attacker lets loose with a straight jab to the face, the defender uses his ankles and knees to pull his hips, and therefore his torso and head as well, out of the range of the punch. Here, the defender uses a rocking movement with his entire body to avoid the punch, simultaneously avoiding the attack and creating the potential for his own forward momentum. His body just out of the attacker's reach, the defender raises his own fist to intercept the attacker's moving arm.

There is no need for the defender to be concerned with power, for the attacking arm provides it. The move is simple, direct, and very difficult for the attacker to counter. As the attacker's arm bounces off the defender's upraised fist, the defender rocks forward to jam any possible follow-up strike and knock the attacker off balance. Again, because this is taijutsu, the defender uses a subtle and graceful rocking from his ankles and knees to provide the knockdown power for his counter.

Approaching Advanced Training

As the years of training progress, the ninja student discovers that the secret to success lies in the ability to keep the attention focused on the goal. Rather than developing new techniques for handling the kicks, punches, and grabs that make up street and field attacks, the advanced student instead works at attuning his natural movements to a wider variety of possible assaults against him. To an outside observer, it actually appears that the ninja's advanced techniques are easier than the beginning techniques.

There is some truth contained in that illusion. As one's skill develops past the point where he or she must *work at* making things happen under pressure, a natural and easy grace seems to emerge as a result. In any endeavor, the professional is one who accomplishes great things with apparent simplicity and ease. In the warrior tradition, this breakthrough is the budding of the development of warrior skills as an art of personal expression.

As an attacker throws a swinging roundhouse kick to the ribs, the defender makes no attempt to protect the target or to block. Instead the defender allows the attacker to commit himself to the kick, and moves in to attack his assailant with a forearm and elbow slam to the head. As the attacker's leg drops to the ground, the defender continues his pivoting advance, throwing his back against the attacker's chest and allowing his trailing arm to lift into a second elbow slam to the attacker's head. With uninterrupted motion, the defender continues to pull back, dragging his arm up and over the attacker's head. As his hand comes into position with a slam to the back of the attacker's head, the defender hooks his free hand beneath the attacker's jaw and continues to rock backward to break his assailant's neck.

As a different method of handling a kick, the author attacks the advancing leg as it moves toward the groin target. The defender's movement is in no way a block or weapon-stopping cover; it is a direct, damaging knee strike to the attacker's moving weapon. Continuing his forward momentum, the defender next allows his leading hand to rise easily, to jam any potential follow-up punches. With a rocking action from his ankles and knees, the defender continues the natural flow of his movements to hammer punches into the attacker's supporting knee and the base of his skull behind the ear.

Against a punching attacker, the author again relies on a direct attack against an exposed weak point. Instead of being lured into a trade-off of techniques by the attacker's initial jabbing punch, the defender simply drops into a position where his face is no longer accessible and executes his own attack. Notice that the defender's body drifts forward as a total unit, pulling his head inside the natural arch of any potential follow-up punch from the attacker's rear hand, thereby reducing again his own accessibility. Note also that the entire body in motion is the source of the defender's power; the punch is not a mere extension of the arm. The attacker's body toppling forward is met with a further extension of the defender's legs, which provides the momentum for a neck-snapping head strike. A punch to the attacker's upper arm and a shin strike to the crotch follow in natural progression, and the defender's forearm slam to the head and leg jam against the attacker's forward knee position the defender for a takedown to end the clash.

In this response to a lunging punch to his lower ribs, the author advances against the attacker's head with an elbow slam. As before, the subtle rocking and angling motions performed from the ankles and knees, and not from the hips, take away all potential targets without the need for blocking or covering actions. With a change in rocking direction set up by the initial move, the defender encounters the attacker's forward momentum with a hand edge strike that knocks the assailant backward. Smooth, flowing actions without hopping or jerking are again the key to mastery.

Progressive Refinement of Subtlety

In the realm of spiritual study, if a concept or practice seems to be elaborately convoluted or in complete contradiction to the natural laws of the universe, there is a great possibility that its true significance has either been lost or is grossly misunderstood. In the realm of self-protection, if a technique seems elaborate or stylized, there is likewise a great possibility that its original martial truth has been lost for generations, or that the entire thing was created by a teacher who was not directly addressing the brutal realities of street or field combat. Contrary to the spirit of challenge and fun so often found in today's training halls is the truth that the more elaborate a technique is, the more likely it is to fail in a high-pressure situation. True enlightened combat methods are so refined and subtle as to appear to be nothing more than well-placed and well-timed body shifts and turns.

Responding to a wrist-grabbing attack and a follow-up punch to the face, the author demonstrates body dynamics that allow the attacker's firm grip to create his own downfall. The student of taijutsu does not have to resort to the dangerous contest of trading punches with the attacker, or descend into an energy-draining wrestling match. Using his legs to generate and maintain movement, the defender simply lowers his arm to cause the attacker to drop.

The insistent attacker holds on tightly, believing that power is the answer to any struggle, so the defender need not use a lot of busy handwork or trapping motions. As the attacker's wrist reaches the ground, his elbow just happens to be lined up with the defender's knee. The attacker generates his own broken elbow as he stiffens and causes the defender to fall forward, driving the kne into the extended joint.

Even more refined is this technique, where the defender times his movements to allow his arm to move away at just the right moment. Fluidly shifting on ankles and knees, the defender slips to a point where he is out of the attacker's range of motion. The attacker, relying on conventional speed, is momentarily taken aback when the target eludes him. As he stiffens to control his forward motion, he runs into the rising shoulder of the defender. The defender glides and turns to let the attacker provide the neck-breaking force to the rising arm and shoulder blow.

Through an intimate knowledge of the physical world, the warrior ultimately gains his entry into the realm of spiritual power.

Even more direct is this third example of possible responses to the wrist grab with follow-up punch. The defender uses relaxed awareness and sensitive timing to pull the attacker forward with the tempting target of his wrist, only to pivot and rock away on his back leg at the last moment. The movement is smooth and continuous, and is not an abrupt jump to the side, which would catch the attacker's attention. The ninja's *kukinage*, or "throw from the energy of the void," is the product of refined sensitivity toward natural harmonic movement, the intentions of others, and the subtleties of body movement, and comes after years of training. So simple as to be beyond the belief of most conventional martial artists, this "throwing without touching" is an example of the purity and directness of the laws of nature in operation.

Text continues from page 65.

"higher art" ninjutsu become progressively refined. As the years of study and experience accumulate, the aware practitioner learns to let go of more and more unnecessary action. The goal is ever the attainment of true economy and naturalness in motion, and the ability to let go of inefficient methods.

New students tend to rely heavily on cruder forms of fighting to accomplish their aims. With a heavy emphasis on strength and speed, the martial artist who has no advanced teacher continues to push the limits that are inherent in any of life's ruts. Bone and muscle do have genetically determined limits, after all. The illusion that speed and power represent the heights of martial arts prowess is the first blinder to be removed on the way toward enlightened movement.

Somewhat more advanced is the concept of increasing the complexity of combination techniques to win through sheer overwhelming performance. This approach to fighting also contains the roots of its own limitations, however, in that the technical fighter must continuously train at top intensity to maintain an edge over advancing age. Any flaw in his health, energy level, or training severity can easily lead to defeat at the hands of a younger, fresher technician.

Only by progressing to the realms of harmonized energy does the warrior begin to glimpse the potential for invincibility. At this advanced stage, strength is no longer matched with raw strength, speed is no longer matched with conventional speed, and technical expertise is no longer matched with complexity of technique. The ninja can fit into his attacker's movements and intentions and use his attacker's very motions to create the attacker's downfall. Dwelling invulnerably in the heart of the danger, the advanced spiritual warrior is in effortless command of his surroundings at all times.

The application of these physical lessons toward understanding the intellectual, emotional, and spiritual confrontations in life are equally as important as gaining an ability to handle physical assailants in threatening situations. A ninja who has progressed to the rarified levels of advanced taijutsu realizes a grander form of effortlessness in accomplishment. Through the insights gained from years of consistent training, he develops the ability to perceive danger as it begins to take form, rather than be restricted to responding once it is on its way to him. Subduing the punch before it flies out, avoiding the blade before it slashes in, and countering the throw before the assailant even comes to grips are the means of exploring his abilities to foresee the future and thereby act accordingly in the present. Through an intimate knowledge of the physical world, the warrior ultimately gains his entry into the realm of spiritual power.

6 REALMS OF CONTENTION
THE SIX ENEMIES AS KEYS TO POWER

I had journeyed to the site of the original Omine Mountain south of Nara. Having taken trains through the heart of Japan's Honshu Island, I traveled from the sophistication of cosmopolitan Tokyo to the rustic beauty of the remote mountain stretches in the center of the Kii Peninsula. Omine has been referred to as the center of shugenja training, the mountain seen as a huge and physical model of the spiritual warrior's mandala. As though passing through a gap in the tight weave of the fabric of time, I had gone from the concrete, glass, and steel of Tokyo to the weathered wood and rice-paper walls of Yoshino in a matter of hours.

In the village of Yoshino, I walked the streets alone just before sunset. I surveyed vista after vista of pine-covered mountain ridges, the sky assuming golden hues with three hawks turning angular loops in front of a salmon-cdgcd bank of evening clouds. At that moment, scores of conch-shell trumpets sounded in unison throughout the peaks and valleys below me. The shugenja who created the haunting, wailing tones were camouflaged completely by the thick green foliage that spread carpetlike down the sides of the mountain. The eerie chords echoed in my heart and left me drained, yet energized at the same time.

As though in a dream I had climbed the winding road to the top of Mount Kimbu, upon which stood the ancient Zaodo, the central sacred place dedicated to the practice of Shugendo. The massive sloping roofed structure had been constructed from the wood of huge cedar trees centuries

The mountain warrior seeker's *shakujo* staff with its six rings representing the six realms through which we wander on the way to enlightened consciousness.

Illustration from a scroll showing shugendo founder En no Gyoja and the denizens of the various realms of influence controlled by Fudo Myoo-oh. Each character is symbolic of humankind's various perceptions of results-producing action in the scheme of universal totality.

before. The weathered wooden staircase that stretched across the entire front of the temple had taken me upward into the dimness of the interior. There inside the cavernous enclosure, wreathed in incense smoke, I had come to stand in front of the towering wooden image of the powerful Kongozaogongen, the guardian spirit of the shugenja of Mount Kimbu. Gripping the three-pointed *sanko* diamond thunderbolt in one hand, the other hand balled into a fist, the symbolic figure had looked down on countless mountain seekers before they had ventured into the wilderness in hopes of finding that last piece of the puzzle, the final experience that would fill in all the empty spaces and bring realization of enlightened consciousness.

I refused to let the falls defeat me, and decided that it was worth experimenting one more time with the power of the shout.

By the time I emerged from the Zaodo, night had fallen. I descended the massive timbers of the staircase to the haunting loneliness of the courtyard that sprawled in front of the temple.

I walked slowly across the deserted expanse, my attention attracted by a dimly lighted staircase that led off to the right of the Zaodo. I followed the winding stairs down past a towering bell shelter. From high inside the structure came the low, rumbling, staccato tones of a lone monk as he chanted the evening's *sutra* between the peals of the huge bronze bell suspended inside.

The bell reverberating into the night behind me, I followed the string of dim light bulbs on down a continuing series of incredibly steep staircases that lead farther and farther into a wood of cedars and ferns. The lighting was a curiosity. I was the only one there, yet the way was lighted well nonetheless.

Twenty minutes later, at the bottom of the long and winding stairway carved into the mountain, I came to a shallow pond that formed the base of an incredibly tall stream of falling water. From unseen heights poured a steady thin sheet of icy silver water that churned the small pond into a foam of noise and spray. I knew immediately what the pond was used for.

I deliberated intensely before the challenge. At last I realized that I could not return home after all these miles without experiencing the shugenja's ordeal by water. Though I had brought no towels or robe for the return trip, I pulled off my clothing and charged into the pond. Before my conventional better judgment could intervene, I headed for the base of the falls.

The water was numbing, so cold and heavy was the flow over my shoulders. The extreme temperature was too much to bear and I moved out from beneath the falls with widely swinging arms working to restore my circulation. I felt foolish and was relieved that there was no one there to witness my lack of determination.

I remembered the jolt of the cold water hitting my body in the depths of the pond back home on my estate in Ohio. On sweltering summer days, my training partners and I would dive into the clear waters after a long and arduous workout. We would always have to shout as we first hit the water. Somehow the shout worked to throw off some of the jolt of the radical change in our energy status. I also remembered a film showing the

Yoshino Village's Zaodo temple, the ancient
spiritual seat of Japan's shugendo tradition
of seeking enlightenment on the sacred
power mountain.

Kimbu Jinja shrine, perched on the steep approach to Omine Mountain, site of shugendo training in the Yoshino region.

yamabushi as they stood in meditation under the icy falls, shouting out in bass voices the mantra of Fudo Myoo-oh. I refused to let the falls defeat me, and decided that it was worth experimenting one more time with the power of the shout.

"Namu Fudo Myoo-oh!" I roared over and over again, believing not so much in the power of the stern divinity, perhaps, but rather in the value of strongly blasted open vowel sounds as a means of moving breath and energy in and out of the body.

It worked, to a degree, but when my concentration dropped even slightly, it was as though the falls themselves had ejected my body. I stood in the pond and considered my annoyance at my perplexing inability.

It was then that I noticed that my feet and lower legs, which had been submerged the entire time that my upper body moved in and out of the water, felt perfectly acclimated to the low temperature. I moved my feet slightly. They were not numb, but were merely used to the cold by this point.

For a third time I moved into the falling water, this time willingly accepting the bone-chilling cold. I made no attempt at either charging or enduring as before, but rather relaxed into the cold wetness. Incredibly, it was as though this were an entirely different waterfall.

My lack of resistance permitted me to stand at ease under the chilling torrent. As with so many other times in my warrior training, it was once again the power of accepting and relaxing that provided the key to overcoming that which seemed to overpower me. How ironic it always was to find that by accepting that which traps one, the trap is found to lose its control over the trapped. So much of opposition is truly in the perception of the beholder.

I left the falls with my own timing, no longer in any particular hurry to be out from under the cascade.

Historically, the seeking of mountainlike power through the enlighten-ment-inducing practices of shugendo began with a ten-step entry into the mountain sanctuary. Each of the ten steps also had a symbolic representa-tion in the six realms of mortal existence and four stages of transcendent existence through which spiritual energy travels on its way from the depths of material world splintered entropy to the heights of cosmic unified oneness. As developed during the Muromachi period of Japanese history (1338–1573), the *Jukkai Shugyo* ten steps of shugendo initiatory training were:

JIGOKU YUKI
"Passage through the hell realm"

The *tokozume* stage began on the first night in the mountains. Initiates were subjected to harsh experience in symbolic form, all the while being coached in the sacred slogan (mantra) and visualization of Dainichi Nyorai, the personification of the concept of universal enlightened wisdom, or what existence would be like if all beings and forces were to attain enlightenment.

GAKI YUKI
"Passage through the starving spirits realm"

The *kiza* portion of the training involved a privately conducted, direct confrontation between the initiate and his mentor, in which the supplicant acknowledged and confessed his personal areas of fear, weakness, and difficulty in maintaining power in life. The mentor was offered a substantial sum of money or gift of value, and the initiate received a transmission of the teachings of Shinpen Daibosatsu, the deified form of shugendo founder En no Gyoja.

*Each of the realms exists as a state of mind that
dictates the manner in which one sees the world,
encounters obstacles, and meets enemies.*

CHIKUSHO YUKI

"Passage through the animal realm"

The next progressive stage of the training focused on the "weighing" of
the initiate's degree of deviation from powerful and purposeful living. The
supplicant's wrists were bound with the cord of his *horagai* (conch-shell
trumpet), and he was read a transmission of means for escaping one's self-
inflicted bindings.

SHURA YUKI

"Passage through the jealous gods realm"

The *mizudachi* portion of the shugendo immersion involved the willful
avoidance of water, as symbolic of all substances that human beings might
feel to be mandatory for maintaining life. No drinking, washing, or bathing
was to be permitted. It is not known how long this period of abstinence
was.

NINGEN YUKI

"Passage through the human realm"

The *aka* stage of the training was entered into on the final night of the
mizudachi portion. The shugenja carried pails to a specially dug well, where
their mentors would douse them with clear water to signify the end of the
water avoidance. In this stage, the water was seen as symbolic of washing
away all worldly hindrances. In conclusion of the rites, each practitioner
was given a power talisman inscribed with his name on it.

TEN YUKI

"Passage through the heavenly realm"

The completion of the *Rokudo*, the first six stages of the training, was
signified with bouts of wrestling referred to as *sumo*, in which one's peers
were faced in the symbolic physical confrontation of man against man.
Following the wrestling, the training entered a new area of emphasis in the
last four of the ten stages.

SEIMON YUKI

"Passage through the *sravaka* (direct disciple of the Buddha) realm"

The *ennen* segment involved ritual movement in the form of a dancelike progression of actions designed to encourage a long and healthy life.

ENGAKU YUKI

"Passage through the *pratyeka* (nonteaching Buddha) realm"

In this stage of the training initiates collect *kogi* sticks for the *goma* sacred fire ceremony. As a part of the ritual, the participants focused their intentions of self-betterment and development of power on the kogi. The ensuing ceremony was seen as a way of burning off past mistakes, power-robbing practices, and weaknesses of the initiates.

BOSATSU YUKI

"Passage through the *bodhisattva* (Buddha-to-be) realm"

The ninth segment of the training sequence involved complete fasting for seven days after a ceremony of drinking specially charged and blessed water.

HOTOKE YUKI

"Passage through the *Buddha* (awakened one) realm"

The tenth and final stage of the historical shugenja's trek through the symbolic physical and spiritual realms was the *shokanjo* ceremony. Clothed in full costume, the initiates would sit in front of their guides and offer a *nyumoku* wood-burning ceremony in acknowledgment of their appreciation.

The historical shugendo progression through six realms of worldly existence and four realms of transcendent existence were a symbolic method of exposing initiates to the concept of individual realms of the *perception* of contention. This same vehicle of six and four realms is also employed in certain sects of religious Mikkyo as well. In everyday life, we each exist in one of the six realms of perception until we have cultivated the enlightened state of mind that allows us to leave behind the limitations of all such realms.

Each of the realms exists as a state of mind that dictates the manner in which one sees the world, encounters obstacles, and meets enemies. So powerful is the allure of each realm over its inhabitants, that individuals from different realms will actually be able to stand side by side at the same

A Tibetan artist's rendering of the wheel of the six symbolic realms of perception in existence.

instant, in the same location, and see the identical physical reality around them, but in radically divergent manners. Just as it is impossible for persons of one realm to experience the reality of others' realms, it is also quite commonplace for a person to find it difficult, if not impossible, to believe that everyone else does not experience life from the perceptions of the outlook of his specific realm.

The "hell realm" is the symbolic title given to the state of mind that causes an individual to be at constant, agonizing opposition with everything that surrounds him. Dwelling in the ghettos of anger, belligerence, and bitterness, the hell being finds threats from the environment lurking around every corner. He thinks he is trapped in his hell forever, and any talk of simply moving to a healthier and happier location is met with rage and firm arguments as to why he is prevented to act by circumstances beyond human control. Every day is a new descent into heartbreak, resentment, and frustration. A sense of anguish is his constant and only companion.

The "hungry spirit realm" is the symbolic title given to the state of mind that causes an individual to be at constant give-and-take battle with his fear of extinction. Dwelling on the outskirts of terror, helplessness, and isolation, the hungry spirit being finds threats from the powers around him a constant goad to more defensive action. He thinks he will have to fight and overcome forever, and any talk of simply studying a bit to better understand the limits of those abstract forces that threaten him is met with skepticism and defensive arguments as to why he is held in his realm of contention by circumstances beyond understanding. Every day is a new exploration into victimization, worry, and powerlessness. A sense of fear is his constant and only companion.

The "animal realm" is the symbolic title given to that state of mind that causes an individual to be at constant battle with the impersonal representatives of nature. Dwelling in the forests of complacency and narrow-mindedness, the animal realm being finds threats from animals, weather, and disease awaiting him from behind every tree. He thinks he is sentenced to his limitations forever, and any talk of simply learning to develop more of a feeling of harmony with the laws of nature is met with bewilderment and resigned statements as to why he is caught in his jungle by circumstances bigger than human capabilities. Every day is a new leap into confusion, restoration of work already accomplished, and toil. A sense of despair is his constant and only companion.

The "human realm" is the symbolic title given to that state of mind that causes an individual to be at constant contention with other human beings in his world. Dwelling in an expanded neighborhood of names, faces, and personalities who single him out from the others, the human realm being finds threats from other individuals no matter where he turns. He thinks he is forced to fight by others, and any talk of simply refusing to rise to every personal confrontation is met with annoyance and attempts at logically explaining why he is the innocent victim singled out by malicious persons who seek to destroy him. Every day is an excursion into committee give-and-take, face reading, and outpsyching. A sense of anxiety is his constant and only companion.

The "jealous gods realm" is the symbolic title given to the state of mind that causes an individual to be at constant contention with everything that seems to threaten all that he has created, built up, and elevated himself to. Dwelling in his mansion of comfort, prestige, and accomplishment, the jealous gods realm being finds threats from envious competitors haunting his every new success. He continuously feels he has yet to attain all that he needs for guaranteed happiness, and any talk of simply relaxing and spending time enjoying all he has already accumulated is met with suspicion and disbelief in the idea that he could possibly have far more than most other people with whom he shares the earth, although from other people's reality he is described as "having it made." Every day is a new sojourn into scanning, plotting, and one-upmanship. A sense of contention is his constant and only companion.

Kongozaogongen, the power figure that appeared to En no Gyoja in a vision, which later became the patron spirit for the shugenja of Kimbu Mountain.

The "heaven realm" is the symbolic title given to that state of mind that causes an individual to relax into the narcotic satisfaction of believing that he has everything luxuriously under control forever. Dwelling in a cloud palace of elegance, leisure, and effortlessness, the heaven being is subtly tricked into the false confidence that accompanies the sense of conviction that he and he alone is responsible for his elevated status, regardless of gifts from fate. He thinks he is ensconced in his heavenly surroundings forever, and any talk of looking for warnings as to troubles taking root under the visible surface of life is met with mild condescension and amusement. Every day is a further drift into illusion and self-deception. Spiritual blindness, a sense of false security, is his constant and only companion.

From each of the symbolic realms emanate perceptions of specific manifestations of an enemy or a conflict:

From the hell realm perspective, the enemy is the environment itself. Freezing in the winters and broiling in the summers, the hell realm perceiver is ever the victim of nameless, faceless, impersonal attackers. His baby is infected by unseen rats, his home and sanctuary are vandalized by inhuman marauders, and his family is consumed by senseless cultural

Yamabushi climbing a jagged rock peak as a test of courage through committed faith.

Once attaining the peak of the mountain, the next test is to endure being suspended over the edge of a cliff and looking down at sure death as a result of any slip in technique or commitment.

brutality that converts children into drug fiends, younger siblings into remorseless killers, and mothers into diseased prostitutes. Everywhere he turns he is confronted by violence, hatred, and aggression, and in anger he retaliates by striking back with more of the same.

From the hungry spirit realm perspective, enemies take the form of shapeless dark forces that stir and swirl about in mockery of the helpless victim. Roaming uninformed and unprotected through life, the hungry spirit realm perceiver is ever the victim of the economic, cultural, and spiritual fears that haunt him relentlessly. His bank account is always a little too drained to permit him to make desperately needed repairs to his home and automobile. His job and career are always at the mercy of corporate and union whims, and his consciousness is filled with dark shapes that seem to tease him with previews of his own death, about which he can do nothing. Everywhere he turns he is confronted by forces that rob him of power and intensify his feelings of helplessness, and in fear he defends himself with tactics that actually call up more of the same fears.

From the animal realm perspective, the enemy takes the form of animals, violent acts of nature, and disease. Parched by droughts and then washed away by floods, the animal realm perceiver is ever the victim of coldly impersonal attackers who just happen upon him and deal out tragedy to

Shugenja submerged in a chilling pool. In addition to work with fire-walking and mountain scaling, the yamabushi mountain seekers also submit themselves to the fears connected with water and body-numbing coldness.

him in the process of attaining their own needs. His crops alone are lost to insects while neighboring farmers prosper, his child is the only one from the group who drowns while swimming in the gravel pit pond, and his life is dominated by those cold, impersonal acts of nature that attack him impassively as he fights back with all his passion and confusion. Everywhere he turns he is confronted by the terrible violence of nature, and in desperation he retaliates by striking back with fist held high against the hurricane.

From the human realm perspective, the enemy is other human beings. Trading fire with the enemy for his government in wartime and hearing his case argued before a jury in peacetime, the human realm perceiver is ever the victim of highly personal attackers. He is confronted by challengers in his place of business, rivals for the love interest in his life, and physical assailants who wish to rob him or cut him down in public places. Everywhere he turns he is confronted by others who scheme to destroy him personally, and with emotional force he strikes out against those persons who move against him, establishing and intensifying rival relationships that further polarize others' views of him.

From the jealous god realm perspective, the enemy takes form as the actions of people and events that threaten to take away all that has already been accumulated. Seeing himself as envied by those who lack what he has and threatening to those who have more, the jealous god realm perceiver is ever the victim of the need to contend against those who have the power to

*All the questions of power have been answered. The
enemies of existence, whatever form they assume, are
quietly recognized as the teachers of the greatest lesson.*

derail what he has set in motion. His home is never large enough, his
business never productive enough, his status never quite established
enough, and he sees his work pirated by others who use to undermine his
position in his field the very success secrets he worked to develop.
Everywhere he turns he is confronted by envy, misunderstanding, and
desire, and in suspicion he retaliates by cutting down threatening competitors with more of the same actions that actually attract competitors.

From the heaven realm perspective, the enemy is the false impression
that one has already eliminated all possible enemies. Warm and snug in the
winters, cool and comfortable in the summers, the heaven realm perceiver
is ever the victim of the false security that carries with it the very seeds of
his inevitable fall from grace. Convinced by his ego needs into believing
that his own power has reached its zenith, he is still haunted by a subtle
emptiness that leaves him looking for something more but unable to find
the fulfillment that he seeks. Everywhere he turns he is reminded of his
power, his control over all aspects of life, and of his chosen and exalted
status. In complacency he carries on unaware of any political, cultural, and
economic changes that billow up on the horizon and promise to take away
all that he has come to believe was granted as his forever.

None of the six symbolic realms is the "best" and none is the "worst."
Each realm has its attraction and is felt to be the best by those who are
caught there. The other realms are seen to be unreal or pitiful. From the
standpoint of enemies, each realm's opposing factors are felt to be the worst
by those who are caught there. The enemies of the other realms are seen to
be unreal or mild in comparison.

The ultimate goal of warrior enlightenment training is to transcend all six
of the realms of limited perception. Upon leaving behind the six realms, one
rises to a state of living in which limits imposed by preconceived ideas
about what one will find in life have vanished. From that point of
transcendence, life becomes a place of freedom and natural harmony. Once
the six are left behind, the concept of enemies also vanishes. From that
point of escaping the need to struggle, those agents that are perceived as
presenting the cause of the struggle also vanish.

This phenomenon has a way of sounding like hollow theory until one
carefully examines life for past fears that no longer exert their haunting

force. So many martial arts practitioners often comment wryly that in their years of holding black belt status, they have never had the opportunity to use their fighting skills on the streets. Before becoming established in their training, however, the events of life often called upon them to handle physical struggles. So many financially successful people often admit that earning well became a simple matter once they discovered their gift. Before acknowledging their inner dreams and gaining the confidence to put them into action, however, those same people often admit that life was a difficult process just making ends meet. By leaving the confines of the given realm of contention, one automatically gives up the old enemies that haunt that realm.

This, therefore, is a part of the grander warrior quest. We begin with taking on small challenges and building up momentum through accomplishment. By advancing through the double-barreled strength of blending experience and awareness, we develop confidence that eventually seasons into wisdom. The challenges become greater and triumphs grow in equal proportion. The challenges become so easy to handle that one finally finds oneself approaching a point of boredom with it all.

This point of near-boredom with success is a highly crucial stage in the ascent to enlightenment. It presents the moment at which one will choose to shift over into a new realm of contention with new enemies and begin the climb all over again, or transcend the concept of struggle-in-life altogether. If one has experienced enough, and developed enough awareness along the way, it is possible to see the truth that the outward manifestations of one's struggles are purely *symbolic* in nature. Struggle itself, whether with humans, the economy, religious torment, or locust plagues, is the lesson, and it provides the means for developing the ability to see that *struggle breeds more struggle*. This realization is the ultimate breakthrough.

This inner experience of the truth of the futility of struggle is what eventually leads to the seeming paradox that *the accomplished warrior is a man of profound peace*. The man who spends enough years with sword in hand eventually comes to the point where all the questions of power have been answered. The enemies of his existence, whatever form they had assumed, are quietly recognized as the teachers of the greatest lesson of the warrior's life. Peace gradually replaces the need for further testing. The sword is replaced with the poet's brush, and the fighter evolves into the philosopher. Such an advancement of the heart is the true and ultimate reward of the warrior's quest for enlightenment.

INDEX